100
THINGS TO DO IN
NEW YORK CITY
BEFORE YOU
DIE

M000314507

100

THINGS TO DO IN
NEW YORK CITY
BEFORE YOU
DIE

2nd Edition

• •

EVELYN KANTER

REEDY PRESS

Copyright © 2019 by Reedy Press, LLC
Reedy Press
PO Box 5131
St. Louis, MO 63139, USA
www.reedypress.com

No part of this publication may be reproduced or transmitted in any form or by any means, electronic or mechanical, including photocopy, recording, or any information storage and retrieval system, without permission in writing from the publisher.

Permissions may be sought directly from Reedy Press at the above mailing address or via our website at www.reedypress.com.

Library of Congress Control Number: 2018962618

ISBN: 9781681061788

Design by Jill Halpin

Printed in the United States of America
19 20 21 22 23 5 4 3 2 1

Please note that websites, phone numbers, addresses, and company names are subject to change or cancellation. We did our best to relay the most accurate information available, but due to circumstances beyond our control, please do not hold us liable for misinformation. When exploring new destinations, please do your homework before you go.

DEDICATION

For the people of NYC,
the most diverse and endlessly interesting in the world,
and to visitors who appreciate all that NYC has to offer.

CONTENTS

• •

Music and Entertainment

● ●

● ●

• •

PREFACE

New York City is the Big Apple, the City that Never Sleeps, Empire City, Fun City, Gotham, and the City of Dreams, all rolled into one.

This is my hometown, and I never tire of sharing its wonders, vitality, history, and ability to set trends that are copied around the world, from entertainment to food and fashion, art and architecture, and oh so many of the world's first this and world's only that.

I grew up in Inwood, at the northern edge of Manhattan, and have lived all my adult life on the Upper West Side, where I raised my two now-adult children as a widowed single mother. Although I've visited some one hundred countries, first as a radio/TV news producer and on-air reporter and then as a travel writer, and have toyed repeatedly with moving to some momentarily interesting city or countryside, I always return, because there's no place like home. It's also where the washing machine is.

Times Square is called the Crossroads of the World, but, really, the entire city deserves that name. More than 175 languages are spoken here by immigrants who chose this place over all others to escape war, poverty, religious discrimination, or some combination of those, and then chose to stay here, as have their descendants. My own parents were just two of the

• •

many millions for whom the Statue of Liberty meant freedom and the promise of a better tomorrow, as it still does today.

The city's four-hundred-year history and importance to the founding of the United States lives on in its names and addresses. Founded by the Dutch, who named it New Amsterdam, the city includes Brooklyn, named for the little brook that flowed through it, and the Bronx, named for the Bronck family, who farmed what is today a king's ransom of real estate that includes the home of baseball's New York Yankees. The city was later captured by the British, who renamed it New York in honor of their duke. You'll find Ft. Tryon Park, now home to the Cloisters, a pantheon to medieval art built by the Rockefellers, who were economic immigrants from Ohio. George Washington took the oath of office as the first US president on what is now Wall Street, in what was then, in 1779, the first US capital city, and long before Alexander Hamilton was a blockbuster Broadway musical star, he lived and worked here. You can visit those places whether or not you see the show.

New York was where the first movies were made, before filmmakers moved to Hollywood, and it's the birthplace of any number of legendary film stars, from Brooklyn's Mae West and Barbra Streisand to Lauren Bacall from the Bronx. It's the chosen home of many others, such as Louis "Satchmo" Armstrong, whose house in Queens has been turned into a museum of jazz. Dozens of TV shows have been set or filmed here, including *All in the Family* and *Blue Bloods*, as you can see at the Paley Center for Media, founded by William S. Paley, who also founded CBS, also located in New York City, of course.

This is also where top chefs and entrepreneurs come to make their name, from Danny Meyer, who started the Shake Shack chain and a hospitality empire from a single hot dog stand in Union Square, to designers such as Diane von Furstenberg and Bronx-born Ralph Lauren, who helped make NYC the fashion capital of the world (sorry, Paris and Milan).

Writing a book limited to just one hundred of the best things to do in the greatest city on the planet is no easy task. It's been both a joy and a frustration to choose only a hundred, when there are at least as many I had to leave out.

• •

ACKNOWLEDGMENTS

Even though I've lived in and explored every part of NYC my entire life, I still don't know everything about it, so thanks to the friends who made so many suggestions about their favorite "you must include this" restaurants, attractions, and events.

Special thanks to the licensed members of the Guide Association of NYC (GANYC) for their recommendations and especially to Andrea Coyle for her assistance.

Thanks also to Nancy Hamilton, author of *100 Things to Do in Fort Myers & Sannibel Before You Die*, for her wise counsel on myriad details.

My biggest thanks are reserved for my son, Gerry, for his patience and support whenever I verbally bit my fingernails.

Credit: Katz's Deli

FOOD AND DRINK

GO TO THE ORIGINAL
SHAKE SHACK

Sure, you could chow down on a whopping, tasty, juicy, cooked-to-order, pure Angus beef burger; a flat-topped hot dog designed to hold toppings in place; crinkle-cut fries designed to keep ketchup from sliding off; or a thick, mixed-to-order shake at a couple of dozen Shake Shack locations in NYC or at one-hundred-plus spots around the world, as far away as Dubai. But nothing beats the original, at the southeast corner of Madison Square Park, where now-legendary restaurateur Danny Meyer grew the biz from a lowly hot dog stand into a shack, and from there into an international empire. Most locations now also serve breakfast. Expect to stand in line just as you would at any other Shake Shack location. Eco-conscious diners will like that the company's menu is hormone and antibiotic free.

23rd St. at 5th Ave.
www.shakeshack.com

LISTEN TO THE PIANO MEN
AT BEMELMANS BAR

Bemelmans is best known for four things—old-fashioned cocktails with modern twists; murals and lampshades painted by the writer and illustrator it is named after; nightly player-vocalists at the Steinway grand, who perform everything from Stevie Wonder to boogie woogie Beethoven; and the megawatt celebrities, such as Paul McCartney and Leonardo DiCaprio, who drop by. Ludwig Bemelmans, author of the "Madeline" children's books, painted the walls and lampshades in the 1940s in exchange for lodging, and the Carlyle Hotel has been smart enough not to mess with them. Vintage dress is not required, but fashionable and appropriate attire is, because you wouldn't want to be denied admission if Jack Nicholson is in the house and watching. Be prepared for a cover charge if you arrive after the music starts at 9 or 9:30 p.m.

35 E. 76th St., 212-744-1600
www.rosewoodhotels.com/en/carlyle

HAIL
THE FOOD HALLS

These food halls are curated gourmet destinations, nothing like suburban mall food courts.

Eataly, founded by now-disgraced chef Mario Batali, is the go-to destination for anything food from Italy, from hand-made pasta to small-batch roasted coffees and olive oils, plus cooking and baking classes. The original multi-story location is on 23rd Street and Fifth Avenue, with a smaller downtown outpost at 4 World Trade Center.

www.eataly.com

The Plaza Food Hall is tucked into the basement of the venerable Plaza Hotel, now sadly less hotel than third-home condo for the world's rich and richer. Find mouth-watering pastries from top chefs such as Daniel Boulud, caviar and lobster, a wine bar, and even a yogurt café with a choice of one hundred toppings.

www.theplazany.com

Essex Street Market is a modern version of the turn-of-the-last-century market that opened in 2018 across the street from the original. Yes, there are butchers and bakers here, but chocolatiers and an herbal apothecary have replaced the candlestick makers.

88 Essex St. at Delancey
www.essexstreetmarket.com

Smorgasburg features only local foods, mostly from Brooklyn-based makers. It's an outdoor foodie fave, open every weekend from April to November and serving up everything from breads to BBQ, all with an appetizing view of the Manhattan skyline. The rest of the year it shares indoor space with Brooklyn Flea.

www.smorgasburg.com

Grand Central Terminal now has two major food courts, both featuring local restaurants, bakeries, and coffee roasters. The Lower Level Dining Concourse provides plenty of seating for quick bites or full meals from more than twenty fast casual vendors. The Market offers meats, cheeses and other ingredients to take home and do it yourself.

www.grandcentralterminal.com

INDULGE YOUR CHEESECAKE CRAVING
AT JUNIOR'S

It doesn't matter whether you call Junior's a restaurant or a diner. It doesn't matter that it serves a full menu of breakfasts, lunches, and dinners. Junior's is synonymous with cheesecake, and has been since the Rosen family opened their first place in downtown Brooklyn in 1950. Maybe they even invented cheesecake. Whatever. Junior's has been serving uncountable huge slabs of creamy, melt-in-your-mouth, sinful deliciousness ever since, with or without fresh strawberry compote on top, along with bagels, burgers, traditional corned beef, and pastrami deli sandwiches. Lately, even Buffalo wings and tuna melts have been added to the menu. The original Brooklyn outpost still serves, and newer locations in the Theater District try to emulate the original via posters and signage.

386 Flatbush Ave. at DeKalb, 718-852-5257
www.juniorscheesecake.com

EAT DINNER WITH GRANDMA
AT ENOTECA MARIA

At Enoteca Maria, half the menu features Italian food, and the other half rotates with cuisines from around the world, depending on who is doing the cooking. Every one of the chefs here is a "nonna," the Italian word for grandma, and whether she is preparing meatballs or shrimp gyoza soup, the result is a meal cooked just for you by a non-professional who simply loves to cook, does it well, and honors her native cuisine. So, it might be an Armenian grandma in the kitchen one day, a Filipino the next, and a Sicilian the day after. The restaurant also offers cooking classes where you can learn how to cook like somebody else's grandma. Reservations are absolutely required for dining or for classes.

27 Hyatt St., Staten Island (steps from the ferry), 718-447-2777
www.enotecamaria.com

PASS THE PICKLES
AT KATZ'S DELICATESSEN

When this place opened in 1888, the neighborhood was dominated by Jewish immigrants from the *shtetls* of Eastern Europe. While Lower East Side demographics have changed greatly since (hint: think Millennials and hipsters), the traditional deli menu has not. There's a welcoming plate of pickles on every table, a mix of "new" (barely pickled) and garlicky full sours that are an ideal complement to hand-cut corned beef and pastrami piled onto overstuffed sandwiches made with crusty rye bread. Matzoh balls are the size of baseballs, and the walls are papered with framed, autographed photos of celebrities and politicians who have eaten here over the years. Just don't ask to be seated at the table from the famous "I'll have what she's having" scene in *When Harry Met Sally*, because the wait staff has heard that request a thousand times too often. This is the real deal deli, including one of the last places in town to serve Dr. Brown's Cel-Ray, a celery-flavored soft drink. Don't knock it until you've tried it.

205 E. Houston St. at Ludlow St., 212-254-2246
www.katzsdelicatessen.com

TIP
You get a ticket when you enter, which is marked with the price of whatever you order, and you pay that total on the way out. Don't lose it, or it could cost you as much as heart bypass surgery.

MORE DELI DELIGHTS

2nd Avenue Deli: This deli moved from the avenue for which it was named when its East Village home became gentrified and rent prices got pickled. Descendants of the founder still serve traditional, over-stuffed, smoked-meat sandwiches, hearty soups, platters of lox (smoked salmon), and knoblewurst, a brat-sized wurst with enough garlic to bring tears to your eyes and to those of your new ex-friends.

1442 1st Ave. and 162 E. 33rd St., www.2ndavedeli.com

Sarge's: Abe "Sarge" Katz opened this deli in 1964, when he retired from the NYPD, and it's been in the same location ever since, serving a traditional deli menu in a location dotted with old-fashioned Tiffany-style lamps and burgundy-brown banquettes. Sit in the back to avoid the large-screen TVs showing sports. Open 24/7/365.

548 3rd Ave., www.sargesdeli.com

Sammy's Romanian: Eating here is like being at a perpetual bar mitzvah or wedding party, where guests sing and dance with friends and strangers in between huge helpings of faves from both Eastern and Western Europe. Go for the signature stuffed cabbage and a schmear of schmaltz (rendered chicken fat) spread on your bread.

157 Chrystie St., www.sammysromanian.com

Ben's Kosher Deli: This is one of the few places left to get beef tongue in a sweet-sour raisin sauce, the way my Bavarian-born mother used to make it, although she never called the sauce "polonaise." Or, just stick with the traditional menu of meat sandwiches and smoked fish platters.

209 W. 38th St. and
211-37 26th Ave., Bayside, Queens, www.bensdeli.net

Pastrami Queen: More luncheonette than deli, with more counter space than table space, serving up tender, smoky pastrami and turkey on Orwashers rye, one of NYC's best bakeries. This has been one of the best-kept Jewish deli secrets for more than twenty years.

78th St. and Lexington Ave., www.pastramiqueen.com

David's Brisket House: There are just three menu choices here: pastrami, brisket, and corned beef. Get yours piled high on a roll or rye bread, with a side of brisket-drippings gravy. Okay, so with sides it's more than three menu items. Fuhgeddaboudit; you get the point. Two Brooklyn locations.

533 Nostrand Ave., Flatbush (original location)
7721 5th Ave., Bay Ridge, www.davidsbriskethouseinc.com

SHARE A STORY WITH O. HENRY
AT PETE'S TAVERN

William Sydney Porter, better known by his pen name, O. Henry, lived next door to Pete's Tavern and spent many hours here, eating, drinking, and writing a story a week for the old *New York World* newspaper, published by Joseph Pulitzer, including O. Henry's best-known short story, "The Gift of the Magi." The booth is well-marked and popular. Pete's Tavern opened in 1864 and has operated continuously ever since, retaining its original decor featuring embossed tin ceilings, stained-glass lighting, and a curved rosewood bar. Literary successors to O. Henry, who died of cirrhosis of the liver in 1910 at age forty-seven, might be sitting here today, writing the next masterpieces on their laptops, Starbucks-style, and working their way through the extensive list of draft beers, seasonal cocktails, burgers, seafood, and pastas.

129 E. 18th St., 212-473-7676
www.petestavern.com

ALTERNATIVE

White Horse Tavern, which dates to the 1880s, became a popular hangout for writers in what were, until the 1930s, the Bohemian days of Greenwich Village. The literary list included James Baldwin, Norman Mailer, Jack Kerouac, and Welsh poet Dylan Thomas, who died shortly after downing eighteen whiskeys here one night. His ghost is said to haunt the place, favoring the table in the corner by his portrait.

567 Hudson St. at 11th St., 212- 989-3956
www.whitehorsetavern1880.com

SAMPLE CLASSIC DIM SUM
AT NOM WAH TEA PARLOR

Small and narrow, on a Chinatown street to match, the Nom Wah Tea Parlor serves dim sum, steamed buns, and egg rolls that are outsized in flavor and prepared to order, which you do by checking off boxes on a small paper form. Prices are low enough to experiment, although it's the rare customer who doesn't like the scallion-dotted pancakes or rice rolls wrapped around boneless bits of spare rib. It's no-frills service and no-ambiance decor, but Nom Wah must be doing something right because it has been doing it successfully since the 1920s. Go early or late to avoid waiting in the street for a table.

13 Doyers St. near Pell St., 212-962-6047
www.nomwah.com

GIMME A SLICE
OF NINETY-NINE-CENT PIZZA

Whether it's a quick mid-afternoon or late-night snack, lunch, or dinner, you can eat fast and cheap at dozens of ninety-nine-cent, $1, and $1.25-a-slice storefronts throughout the city, all operating under similar names but not necessarily related. While these are not gourmet wood-fired pizzas, they are tasty, and you can add pepperoni or veggies and a soda for another buck. Because of the sheer volume, your slice or whole pie is always fresh out of the oven and bubbling hot. Expect to stand at a counter to eat, or take your take-out home or to the office. If you choose one of the ninety-nine-cent slice shops in the Theater District, you can expect a line, often out the door, between 10:30 and 11 p.m., after the final curtain.

SEE BROADWAY STARS
AT SARDI'S

A Theater District landmark for a couple of generations, these days Sardi's is celebrated less for its food than for its walls, papered with hundreds of framed caricatures of Broadway shows and show people. The menu tends to be over-priced and under-flavored, so skip lunch or dinner and opt instead for a drink at the bar. You still get to enjoy the museum-quality artwork by legendary illustrator Al Hirschfeld, and your eyesight should be intact enough even after a refill or two to find the not-so-hidden lines in each portrait honoring his daughter, Nina, by name.

234 W. 44th St., 212-221-8440
www.sardis.com

FIND YOUR SEVENTH HEAVEN
AT THE QUEENS FOOD CRAWL

Queens is the most multi-ethnic borough of NYC, and the #7 subway line is its main street. There are at least a dozen family-owned restaurants within a three-block walk of any station, and it's tough to make a bad choice at any one of them. Greek tavernas are plentiful in Astoria, around the Queensboro Plaza stop. The Roosevelt Avenue stop is often called Little Manila, with a cluster of Filipino restaurants. Little Korea is around the 69th Street stop. NYC's Tibetan and Colombian populations center in Elmhurst, so the 74th Street stop offers hand-torn noodle soups and butter tea, along with arepas (corn pancakes) and plantains. If you stay on the train to the end-of-the-line Flushing Main Street stop, you will be rewarded with Malaysian, Chinese, and Indian dishes.

MAKE IT MEDIUM RARE
AT PETER LUGER STEAK HOUSE

Johnny Carson is just one of many celebrities and mere mortals who have rated this as the top steakhouse in NYC, maybe the planet. That includes Zagat's guide to the top restaurants, which has proclaimed it number one for thirty-plus years in a row. Maybe it's because Luger's butchers the cows and dry-ages the beef in-house, which helps make its famous sliced porterhouse-for-two fork tender, or because its unpretentious German beer hall atmosphere has remained unchanged since it opened in 1887. All of those, plus traditional sides such as creamed spinach and desserts such as apple strudel, make it a truly classic NYC dining experience. Beware: its no-nonsense waiters just might sneer if you order anything other than medium rare, and Luger's lacks trendy "mixologists" for crafting your cocktails. Debit cards and cash are accepted, but not credit cards. The good news: there's an ATM across the street.

178 Broadway at Driggs Ave., Brooklyn, 718-387-7400
www.peterluger.com

MORE GREAT PLACES TO FIND THE BEEF

Old Homestead has been in the Meatpacking District since 1868, before it turned into trendy Meapo. While modern menu items such as lobster rolls have been added, the stars here are still steak and burgers, including Kobe beef, served amidst decor best described as Victorian bordello.

56 9th Ave. at 15th St., 212-242-9040
www.theoldhomesteadsteakhouse.com

Gallaghers is another steakhouse that dry-ages its own beef, displayed in a see-through glass refrigerator. This popular Theater District dining spot has been around since 1927.

228 W. 52nd St., 212-586-5000
www.gallaghersnysteakhouse.com

DRINK SOME HISTORY
AT MCSORLEY'S OLD ALE HOUSE

McSorley's has been at the same location in the East Village since 1854 and hasn't changed its decor since. The old wide-plank wooden floor creaks beneath your feet, and the walls are cluttered with museum-quality memorabilia, including an original "wanted'" poster for Abraham Lincoln's assassin. Honest, Abe was here once, and John Lennon stopped in more than once. The long wooden bar has been burnished to a deep shine by generations of elbows resting on it between sips of the pub's own amber McSorley's Ale, which used to be brewed in the basement. The suds are served in half-pint glasses, so order a couple at a time if you're really thirsty. If you down too many, you'll be using the unisex bathroom, designed at a time when women were not permitted to enter such joints. It didn't become co-ed until a 1970 Supreme Court ruling forced the issue.

15 E. 7th St. between 2nd and 3rd aves. 212-473-9148
mcsorleysoldalehouse.nyc

EAT EASTERN EUROPEAN SOUL FOOD
AT VESELKA

A Lower East Side institution since it opened in 1964, Veselka is celebrated for its old-fashioned prices and huge portions of rib-sticking Eastern European food, served twenty-four/seven. Regulars favor the *bigos*, a hearty stew of pork, kielbasa, sauerkraut, and onions; the housemade *pierogies* (dumplings); or the stuffed cabbage, filled with meat or mushrooms. The breakfast menu is fluffy with omelettes, pancakes, and delicate cheese-filled blintzes. Veselka is popular with budget-challenged college kids from nearby NYU and with the after-theater and late-night clubbing crowd, who come for the food and not for the dated decor, which favors chipped Formica tables.

144 2nd Ave. at 9th St., 212-228-9682
www.veselka.com

TRY TWENTY-ONE DAYS OF PRIX FIXE:
NYC RESTAURANT WEEK

What started in the '90s as a way to generate business in the dead days after the Christmas holidays, after the tourists went home and when NYC residents stayed home, has turned into a foodie festival copied by cities around the world, from Albuquerque to Zagreb. More than three hundred top NYC restaurants participate with three weeks of affordable three-course prix fixe lunches priced in the $20s and dinners priced in the $30s. Watch for the winter event the last ten days of January and first ten days of February (and the summer version the last part of July and first part of August). It's a chance to sample a famous and expensive restaurant you otherwise might not be able to afford, or to return to one that nearly broke your bank account on a full-price visit.

FAB FACT

NYC Restaurant Week gave birth to French Restaurant Week, occurring during the two weeks surrounding Bastille Day on July 14. Prix fixe meals are $17.79, in honor of the year of the French Revolution.

TIPS

Lunch reservations are easier
to get than dinner reservations.
Mid-week reservations are easier to get
than weekend ones.

Restaurant Week is promoted by NYCGO, the
city's member-supported tourism agency, and
only dues-paying members can participate
in Restaurant Week. Find your dining
destination of choice on its website but
make your reservation directly with
the restaurant or via OpenTable.

GET THE ROYAL TREATMENT
AT JONES WOOD FOUNDRY

The owners of Jones Wood Foundry are mum about whether the former Meghan Markle or hubby Prince Harry have stopped here for a taste of British comfort food, but you certainly can.

It's not just classic Scotch eggs, Yorkshire pudding, beer-battered fish and chips, and shepherd's pie, because there's also a seasonal farm-to-table menu with modern and international influences. This pub (street level) and restaurant (downstairs) is named for the iron foundry that was on this site in the late 1800s, forging staircases, doors, and even manhole covers for a growing New York City.

401 E. 76th St. between 1st and York aves., 212-249-2700
www.joneswoodfoundry.com

ALTERNATIVE
There's a similar menu, and the option of prix fixe lunch or dinner, at The Shakespeare, 24 E. 39th St., www.theshakespearenyc.com.

FEEL LIKE A MILLION
AT THE CAMPBELL

Just steps away from the hustle and bustle of the Grand Central Terminal concourse is a time warp of quiet elegance, with wood-paneled walls, soaring leaded-glass windows, a hand-painted ceiling, and a walk-in fireplace large enough to spit-roast a Wall Street bull or bear. This was the private office of millionaire John W. Campbell, who helped buddy Cornelius Vanderbilt build and run his New York Central railroad (predecessor to MetroNorth). Its opulence as an after-work escape is matched only by the difficulty of finding the entrance, which helps keep it semi-secret. Drinks are primarily old-fashioned classic cocktails, plus a decent wine list and bar bites menu. Everything is pricey, but for the extravagance you'll feel like a Gilded Age tycoon or Don Draper from *Mad Men*.

15 Vanderbilt Ave., 212-297-1781
www.thecampbellnyc.com

MANGIA
AT THE FEAST OF SAN GENNARO

The largest of NYC's ethnic festivals takes over Little Italy and parts of Chinatown for ten days each September, with music, cooking demonstrations, carnival rides, and food. Lots and lots of food. More than two hundred vendors, mostly from the neighborhood's most famous restaurants, serve up heaping helpings of everything from pizza and sausage and peppers to zeppoles and more flavors of gelato than you knew existed. All of it is designed to honor the patron saint of Naples.

Centered on Mulberry St., spilling over onto Grand and Mott
www.sangennaro.nyc

ALTERNATIVE

The Brooklyn version is the Giglio Feast, another ten-day street fair distinguished by several massive, elaborate towers carried by hundreds of locals who march through Williamsburg, commemorating the story of San Paolino, a bishop who was kidnapped in 410 AD in Italy. The largest is an eighty-foot tower at whose base a brass band plays Italian ditties, including the *Rocky* theme. All that exertion requires nightly feasts of street food.

www.olmcfeast.com

SCREAM FOR ICE CREAM
AT THE AMPLE HILLS' RED HOOK FACTORY

What began as a single scoop shop with quirky hand-made flavors and equally quirky mix-ins concocted in the back of the store has turned into an impressive success story, with a factory able to churn out two hundred gallons of ice cream an hour. The benefit of getting your ice cream fix at Ample Hills' Red Hook factory is that you can watch the process through a glass window. Production is monitored by the husband-wife team, Brian Smith and Jackie Cuscuna, who started it all, creating flavors linked to local history. One is The Hook, a burnt-sugar ice cream with chunks of salted fudge, honoring a former sugar factory next door and the salty sea air at the doorstep. There are also several Ample Hills scoop shops around the home borough of Brooklyn and beyond, plus seasonal ice cream stands in NYC parks and at Atlantic Ocean beaches.

421 Van Brunt St., 718-875-1273
www.amplehills.com

FIND FRESHIES
AT UNION SQUARE GREENMARKET

A farmers' market in the middle of Manhattan? Absolutely.
The city's first modern greenmarket opened in Union Square in
1976, the year of America's two-hundredth birthday. Besides
growing in popularity over the years, it's given birth to dozens
of farm-to-table greenmarkets throughout town. This is still
the biggest, where one-hundred-plus local (within one hundred
miles) farmers, fishmongers, butchers, bakers, cheesemakers,
and florists take over Union Square Park plaza every Monday,
Wednesday, Friday, and Saturday year-round. Here's where to
buy—in season—sweet corn or heirloom tomatoes picked that
morning, grass-fed beef, hydroponic herbs, gluten-free breads,
homemade pickles and jams, fragrant lavender, house-smoked
sausages, wheatgrass juice, honey, and more. In keeping with
the green theme, bring your own bag—preferably canvas, not
plastic—and fill it up with farm freshness.

E. 17th St. between Broadway and Park Ave. South, 212-788-7476
www.grownyc.org

GET A KISS
AT THE CHOCOLATE MUSEUM

The full name The Chocolate Museum and Experience with Jacques Torres doesn't exactly melt in your mouth, but the bonbons from the city's top chocolatier most certainly do. Exhibits inform visitors about the cultural and economic history of chocolate, and there are chocolate sculptures, including one of the NYC skyline. For many, especially kids, the real treat is the multiple tastings, including a traditional spiced Mayan hot chocolate prepared with beans ground by hand on the premises. There's also a shop and café. Torres, who calls himself Mr. Chocolate, has several other shops in Manhattan and Brooklyn, but this is the only museum to chocolate.

350 Hudson St. at King St., 917-261-4252
www.mrchocolate.com

EAT GREAT ITALIAN
ON ARTHUR AVENUE

While Manhattan's Little Italy has changed significantly over the generations, Arthur Avenue in the Bronx has not. It's still bursting at the seams with more than a dozen family-owned restaurants, perhaps with a real Italian grandmother at the stove, and a couple of dozen shops laden with eye-popping varieties of sausages, cheeses and prosciuttos, fresh meats and seafood, and fresh handmade pastas and pastries. Many are housed inside the Arthur Avenue Retail Market, created by beloved NYC mayor Fiorello La Guardia in the 1940s to improve sanitation by bringing pushcarts indoors. This is where Dion DiMucci grew up, naming his '50s rock-and-roll group, Dion and the Belmonts, after the neighborhood's main street. This is also where Joe Pesci was working as a maitre d' when another Italian guy named Robert De Niro discovered his comic charm. Remember Pesci in *My Cousin Vinny*?

www.arthuravenuebronx.com

TIP

The website www.arthuravenuefoodtours.com offers private and group tours focusing on shopping and eating. Mostly eating.

EXPLORE RESTAURANT ROW:
FORTY-SIXTH STREET

The block of 46th Street between Eighth and Ninth avenues, at the edge of the Theater District, is lined with old-fashioned brownstones, and nearly every one contains a restaurant on the ground floor or in the basement. Most have happy hours before the shows start, and many feature live music after. Theater folk are known to hang out in Joe Allen; fans of paella head to Meson Sevilla; craft beer enthusiasts can choose Bourbon Street or the rowdy House of Brews; and venerable Barbetta is known to attract those with the palate and wallet for fine dining, Northern Italian cuisine, elegant decor that includes flowers on every table, and a backyard garden. Or, skip the theater and spend the evening dining and dancing to a live swing or jazz band every night of the week at Swing 46.

www.restaurantrownyc.com

MAKE MIDDLE EASTERN MAGIC
AT SAHADI'S

Open barrels, burlap bags, and bins brimming with dozens of kinds of olives, grains, beans, spices, dried fruits, nuts, and fresh-roasted coffee tempt all the senses, most especially those of taste and smell. Homemade flatbreads, baklava, and other pastries dotted with pistachio bits and slathered with honey crowd the bakery counter. Offering more than just Old World charm, this is a gourmet grocery shop specializing in Middle Eastern fare you don't find in the average grocery store. Sahadi's has been operated by the same family since 1948, when it was opened by Lebanese immigrants, and has been in the same location on Brooklyn's Atlantic Avenue ever since.

187 Atlantic Ave., 718-624-4550
www.sahadis.com

SPLURGE ON FINE FRENCH DINING
AT LE BERNARDIN

A perennial on the list of the world's best restaurants, this gem from star chef Eric Ripert and partner Maguy Le Coze is known for its service, presentation, and extensive wine list. But it's the ethereal menu, focusing on seafood, that keeps earning it Michelin stars. Instead of appetizers and mains, the menu is divided into the unusual headings of "almost raw" dishes such as tuna carpaccio, "barely touched" options such as rare smoked sea trout, and "lightly cooked" dishes such as steamed black bass with a zingy bitter orange-lemongrass bouillon. There's a set four-course menu ($160 at press time), which includes dessert. You're in luck when maple-roasted figs with Tahitian vanilla ice cream are on the menu. If the prix fixe is above your pay grade, get a less expensive taste of those culinary award stars in the lounge and soak up the atmosphere with Peruvian-style ceviche and a glass of wine.

155 W. 51st St., 212-554-1515
www.le-bernardin.com

HAVE A RELIGIOUS EXPERIENCE
AT JOHN'S OF TIMES SQUARE

At John's of Times Square, thin-crust pizzas are cooked to order in eight-hundred-degree, coal-fired brick ovens, with a traditional, eight-slice pie serving up to four people. There's also a long list of pasta dishes and salads, and the calamari appetizer portion is generous enough for a meal. Bigger eaters can *mangiano* on the hearty spaghetti with meat sauce. But the real appeal is that this restaurant in the heart of the Times Square Theater District is housed in a former church, which has retained the original stained-glass windows, so you could call eating here a religious experience. Warning: Only whole pizza pies are sold, so do not embarrass yourself by asking for slices.

260 W. 44th St., 212-391-7560
www.johnspizzerianyc.com

MUSIC AND ENTERTAINMENT

KICK UP A STORM
AT RADIO CITY MUSIC HALL

The world-famous Radio City Christmas Spectacular has been staged annually since 1933, and everybody should see it at least once in their lives for the extravagant sets and the precision high-kicking dancing of the Rockettes, including the favorite "Dance of the Wooden Soldiers." Another treat is to go behind the scenes of this Art Deco gem when the massive 1.8 million cubic foot auditorium is empty. A backstage tour visits lounges and other areas that are off-limits to theater-goers. Chat with a Rockette to learn what her day is like and ask how many pairs of dance shoes she wears out in a year. Tours are every thirty minutes, 9:30 a.m. to 5 p.m. daily.

6th Ave. at 50th St.
www.msg.com/venue-tours/radio-city-music-hall

BE MY VALENTINE
AT THE TIMES SQUARE VOW RENEWAL

Of course you could join one million of your closest friends for the world's largest New Year's Eve party in Times Square. But it's much more intimate and romantic to renew your vows here, or actually be married here, on Valentine's Day. Join other couples, hetero or not, young or not, New Yorkers or not, on the famous Red Steps for a giant love-in to say "I do" all over again. All couples are welcome, whether you've been hitched for one year or fifty.

www.timessquarenyc.org

GRAB A PARTNER
AT MIDSUMMER NIGHT SWING

For three weeks each summer, Lincoln Center's Damrosch Park is covered with a dancer-friendly wooden floor to become an outdoor dance club, with live bands and dancing under the stars. Although the many variations of swing dominate, including '40s Big Band, blues, '50s Lindy hop, and country honky tonk, all types of dance music are represented, a different one each night, so you can also tango, salsa, or show off your tricked-out hip-hop moves. A free lesson is included with each ticket (under $20), but many sit around outside the dance floor to enjoy the music and dance on the concrete park plaza for free.

June/July in Damrosch Park
www.lincolncenter.org

After a few days to reset the furniture, the following three weeks is the **Lincoln Center Out of Doors** festival, with free music and dance performances, film screenings, and poetry readings.

July/August in Damrosch Park

Then, it's time for the **Metropolitan Opera Summer HD** series, when live-to-film broadcasts are shown outdoors on a gi-normous screen that covers the facade of the Met Opera House, with culture fans filling the three thousand chairs set up in the plaza.

Broadway at 66th St.
www.lincolncenter.org

INDULGE IN
IAMBIC PENTAMETER
AT SHAKESPEARE SONNET SLAM

The world-famous Public Theater performances of Shakespeare plays in Central Park each summer aren't the only game in town. There's also Shakespeare in Bryant Park, and the chance to celebrate the Bard's birthday each April with readings of all 154 Shakespeare sonnets, in order, at the Naumburg Bandshell in Central Park. Professional actors, who have included Stacy Keach and Richard Thomas, and talented amateurs take turns in this three-hour celebration of iambic pentameter.

www.shakespearesonnetslam.com

PULL SOME STRINGS
AT THE SWEDISH COTTAGE
MARIONETTE THEATRE

This 1876 wooden schoolhouse was moved to Central Park by co-designer Frederick Law Olmsted to offer nature exhibits for kids. Since 1947, it's been home to one of the last marionette theater companies in the United States, where puppeteers stage whimsical musical productions of such classics as *Peter Pan*, *Cinderella*, and *Hansel and Gretel*, along with original content featuring snowmen, bears, talking twigs, and other kid-pleasing characters. Best of all, tickets are an affordable $10 or less, the Central Park Carousel is just a short walk, and the Central Park Zoo is a slightly longer walk.

www.centralparknyc.org

CELEBRATE THE SILVER SCREEN
AT THE TRIBECA FILM FESTIVAL

What started as a small effort by local resident and business owner Robert De Niro to drum up business for Lower Manhattan restaurants and shopkeepers in the dark days after 9/11 has turned into an internationally recognized showcase for independent films, especially documentaries. Since 2002, it has expanded with panel discussions featuring celebrities in film, art, and music, plus concerts, comedy shows, a street fair, and more. There are now so many events that the festival is three weeks long and spread over multiple locations throughout Manhattan, including an old movie theater De Niro purchased and renamed Tribeca Cinema, which shows independent films year-round. Tickets for the September film festival start selling—and selling out— in spring because of its history of showing both international premieres and restored classics along with the occasional major studio premiere, such as *Spider-Man 3*.

www.tribecafilm.com

DRAG YOURSELF
INTO LIPS

Lips has the look and feel of an elegant, old-fashioned supper club, and the showgirl costumes are straight out of a Flo Ziegfeld extravaganza or Busby Berkeley movie musical. This is NYC's longest-running drag show, where the—er—ladies of Lips vamp and vogue in impossibly high heels, extra-long eyelashes, and ceiling-scraping headdresses, sometimes impersonating legendary musical icons, sometimes inviting the audience to join drag karaoke. The entertainers shake and shimmy their way onto guests' laps, even serving your dinner and drinks. It's always good fun, and a great place to celebrate a birthday, mortgage burning, bachelor or bachelorette party, or your most recent divorce.

227 E. 56th St., 212-675-7710
www.lipsnyc.com

GET JAZZED UP
IN GREENWICH VILLAGE

John Coltrane, Dave Brubeck, and Ahmad Jamal are alive and well—or at least their musical legacy is—in the legendary jazz joints that have been around for the better part of a century and in newer jazz clubs, all of which attract a new generation of aficionados.

Smalls, 183 W. 10th St., 212-252-5091
www.smallsjazzclub.com

Village Vanguard, 178 7th Ave., 212-255-4037
www.villagevanguard.com

Blue Note, 131 W. 3rd St., 212-475-8592
www.bluenotejazz.com

Dizzy's Club Coca-Cola: Named for Dizzy Gillespie, featuring the Jazz at Lincoln Center Orchestra led by Wynton Marsalis.

In the Time Warner Center, Columbus Circle
www.jazz.org

Birdland: Haven for great jazz artists, including Kurt Elling, and performers, including Aaron Neville. Sundays belong to the resident Afro-Latin Jazz Orchestra.

315 W. 44th St., 212-581-3080
www.birdlandjazz.com

Smoke Jazz & Supper Club: A popular old-fashioned jazz and blues joint in a residential neighborhood, with comfy sofas that make for a living room feel and a rotating roster of internationally known and upcoming local artists.

2751 Broadway at 105th St., 212-864-6662
www.smokejazz.com

How did NYC become known as the Big Apple? There are two stories. Believe whichever one you like.

BIG APPLE LEGEND #1

The nickname is from 1920s jazz musicians, whose slang for a job or gig was "apple." NYC, being the center of the jazz universe with the biggest paycheck for a job or a gig, was referred to as the "big apple."

BIG APPLE LEGEND #2

The nickname is from sports reporter John Fitz Gerald, also in the 1920s, whose beat was the racetrack and who heard stable hands refer to gigs or jobs as apples, and to NYC as the "big apple" because it paid better than small-town apples. This version claims Fitz Gerald began publishing the term in his columns, which were read by jazz musicians who played the horses between gigs and who adopted it.

FOR A TRIVIA CONTEST

In 1673, the Dutch captured NYC from the British and dubbed it New Orange, in honor of William of Orange. However, the following year the city reverted to English control and its former name, New York, in honor of the Duke of York. Originally, of course, the city was founded by the Dutch and called New Amsterdam, honoring the largest Dutch city, which nobody ever has called the Big Cheese. Is your head spinning now? Go eat a big apple, because an apple a day keeps the psychotherapist away.

JOIN THE AUDIENCE
AT LATE-NIGHT TV SHOWS

All the late-night TV shows worth watching are taped in NYC, and tickets are both free and relatively easy to get, so long as you request them at least six weeks ahead. An alternative is day-of-show standby tickets, usually handed out around noon at the studio where the show is taped.

The Tonight Show Starring Jimmy Fallon
www.nbc.com/the-tonight-show/tickets/main

Late Show with Stephen Colbert
www.cbs.com/shows/the-late-show-with-stephen-colbert

Saturday Night Live (SNL)
Email request to snltickets@nbcuni.com in August only,
for the September-May season.

Daily Show with Trevor Noah
www.cc.com/shows/the-daily-show-with-trevor-noah

Last Week Tonight with John Oliver
www.lastweektickets.com

Late Night with Seth Meyers
www.nbc.com/late-night-with-seth-meyers

SNAG CHEAP CURTAINS
AT 20AT20

While the Broadway Week half-price ticket deal gets all the front-page headlines, there's an even better bargain for Off-Broadway shows. Around the same time as Broadway Week, which is really three weeks in January/February and three weeks in July/August, 20at20 requires nothing more than showing up at the ticket window twenty minutes before the show to get a $20 ticket. Best bets are weekdays and matinees, for long-running hits such as *Stomp*, and newer offerings.

www.20at20.com

LAUGH IT UP
AT UPRIGHT CITIZENS BRIGADE

The city's only accredited improvisational and sketch comedy school has trained writers for top TV shows, along with any number of their actors, plus stand-up comedians. Alums who got their start here include Amy Poehler, Kate McKinnon, and Aziz Ansari. There are improv shows year-round by students and recent grads in the school's own club in Hell's Kitchen and an outpost in the East Village. You'll laugh a lot, including all the way to the bank, because tickets are laughably cheap (at press time, that was $5-$12).

555 W. 42nd St., 212-366-9176
www.ucbtheatre.com

FIND FREE PERFORMANCES
AT THE LIBRARY FOR THE PERFORMING ARTS

This New York Public Library branch within Lincoln Center is home to a treasure trove of theater and ballet memorabilia and exhibits on NYC theatrical icons, from Rodgers and Hammerstein to Jerome Robbins. Also always free are regular performances and concerts, including by graduates of the the Juilliard School in Lincoln Center, and film screenings.

www.nypl.org/events/programs/lpa

SEE WHERE STARS ARE BORN
AT APOLLO THEATER

The Apollo, as everybody calls it, bills itself as the theater "where stars are born and legends are made," and that's not hype. Back in 1934, a nervous teenager named Ella Fitzgerald took the stage of the newly named Apollo Theater for Amateur Night, one of the first winners of many to follow, including Jimi Hendrix and a group called the Jackson Five. They proved so popular that they were brought back the next season to open for Etta James ("At Last") and the Coasters ("Speedoo"). The Apollo was at the heart of the Harlem Renaissance of the '30s and '40s, and in the '50s and '60s it helped launch the careers of Marvin Gaye, Diana Ross, Stevie Wonder, Michael Jackson, and Aretha Franklin, a nineteen-year-old prodigy who made her first NYC appearance here in 1962 with the Count Basie Review. Wednesdays are Amateur Night, when you can see tomorrow's superstars.

253 W. 125th St., 212-531-5300
www.apollotheater.org

ALTERNATIVE

From 1943 until his death in 1971, Louis "Satchmo" Armstrong lived in a modest home in Corona, Queens. Now a National Historic Landmark, it's filled with memorabilia of his career, and there are jazz afternoons and soirees in the garden.

Louis Armstrong House
34-56 107th St., 718-478-8274
www.louisarmstronghouse.org

EXPLORE CARNEGIE HALL'S MUSICAL HISTORY
AT THE ROSE MUSEUM

One of NYC's best secrets is the Rose Museum, tucked inside the office building adjoining Carnegie Hall, the 1881 building built by Andrew Carnegie and saved from demolition in 1960 by violinist Isaac Stern. Photos, programs, and artifacts of its famous musicians are displayed, from opening night with Tchaikovsky conducting to more recent performances by the Beach Boys. Arturo Toscanini's baton and Benny Goodman's clarinet share the spotlight with album covers of musical icons who recorded live performances here, including Judy Garland, Harry Belafonte, and Duke Ellington, whose signature composition, "Take the A Train," is about the subway that links Harlem (125th Street stop) and Carnegie Hall (59th Street stop).

154 W. 57th St.
www.carnegiehall.org
Closed mid-July to mid-September.

PAY $2.75 A TICKET
FOR MUSIC UNDER NEW YORK

Hear opera, Andean music, rock-and-roll classics, jazz, and more in eighty NYC subway stations, performed by 350 talented local soloists and small groups who audition and compete for the right to perform with the MTA's Music Under New York program. The most coveted spot is the Times Square station, in the hallway between the #1/2/3 and #7 trains, both for its acoustics and for the foot traffic that generates selfies and tips, including for performers' CDs, which have been vetted like the musicians. There are plenty of other subway performers, too, because anybody can whip out a saxophone or bang on a plastic bucket on a platform, or take over in a moving subway car while doing a trapeze act with passenger handrails to the beat of a blasting boombox. Better to give your money to the legit, vetted performers than the freelance hustlers.

web.mta.info/mta/aft/muny

PLAY IT AGAIN, SAM
AT FILM FORUM

Megaplexes playing big-budget blockbusters aren't the only game in town. Since 1970, when it opened with folding chairs for seating, Film Forum has been the place for vintage classics, from Buster Keaton films to *Casablanca* to Akira Kurosawa films and documentaries, including ones about urban planner Jane Jacobs and polka-dot artist Yayoi Kusama. The theater has managed to outlive the demise of NYC's other indie film houses, and a recent multi-million-dollar make-over has modernized it from seedy to stadium-style seating. Saturday mornings are for kids, but grownups also have been known to enjoy old and older faves such as *Yellow Submarine* or the timeless slapstick of Charlie Chaplin or Abbott and Costello.

209 W. Houston St., 212-727-8110
www.filmforum.org

SEE SUPERSTARS
PERFORM
AT THE GLOBAL CITIZEN FESTIVAL

The biggest annual outdoor concert of the year, held each September on Central Park's Great Lawn, also features the biggest names in music. Janet Jackson, John Legend, and Janelle Monáe headlined in 2018, and Beyoncé, Ed Sheeran, Coldplay, and Metallica in previous years. It's part music festival and part social activism festival, designed to raise awareness on a range of issues, from climate change to human trafficking, while working to eliminate extreme poverty by 2030. Concert tickets are free but must be earned by completing small tasks, such as emailing an elected official and posting about positive global citizenship on social media. There are similar Global Citizen concerts in other cities around the world, supporting the same world causes.

www.globalcitizen.org

DON'T RAIN ON MY PARADE:
BALLOONFEST

For many New Yorkers and holiday visitors, the best part of the annual Macy's Thanksgiving Day Parade is the night before, watching the world-famous parade balloons get inflated with helium and pop into life one leg, arm, or hat at a time. This happens on the streets around the American Museum of Natural History, where the parade starts. Balloons such as Kermit the Frog, Charlie Brown, Sonic the Hedgehog, Buzz Lightyear, Snoopy, Garfield, Angry Birds' Red, *Ice Age*'s Scrat, Hello Kitty, Shrek, and Abby Cadabby start taking shape in the early afternoon. Inflation is open to the public through mid-evening.

TIP

Viewing spots along the sidewalks between 76th Street and 59th Street along Central Park West are generally less crowded than on Sixth Avenue between 59th and 38th streets, although less crowded means five deep instead of ten.

www.macys.com/parade

SPORTS AND RECREATION

GO FISH
AT SEAGLASS CAROUSEL

Unlike traditional carousels with horses and other familiar land creatures, this whimsical merry-go-round is full of fish. Climb into the belly of one to spin slowly around on an axis while the carousel turns for non-stop movement that feels like floating along in fast-moving water. Instead of calliopes playing stirring band music, the soundtrack here is more appropriate sea sounds, and the changing lights on the otherwise colorless fiberglass fish combine to induce a trancelike state of joy and wonder. Just look for the seashell-shaped, glass-walled building in Battery Park, close to the water creatures that inspired it.

212-344-3491
www.seaglasscarousel.nyc

MORE NYC CAROUSELS TO TRY

MANHATTAN

Central Park Carousel: The granddaddy of New York City merry-go-rounds. When it opened in 1873, it was powered by a mule, and it has been powered by happy kids ever since.

Mid-park at 64th St., centralparknyc.org

Le Carousel: Enjoy French cabaret music with your ride at this Victorian-style carousel in Bryant Park.

6th Ave. at 40th St., www.bryantpark.org

BROOKLYN

Jane's Carousel: It's hard to match the views from this seaside ride in DUMBO (Down Under the Manhattan Bridge Overpass), in a Jean Nouvel glass pavilion. This classic carousel was built in the 1920s during the heyday of carousel popularity and was moved here from its original location in Youngstown, Ohio, and beautifully restored and named for one of its philanthropic benefactors.

Brooklyn Bridge Park, www.janescarousel.com

Prospect Park Carousel: With horses carved long ago by Charles Carmel, this is another vintage gem, located near the Willink entrance at Flatbush Avenue and Empire Boulevard.

Prospect Park, www.prospectpark.org

B&B Carousel: This one dates from 1906 and is a perennial Coney Island favorite, with fifty hand-carved horses and two grand chariots, located in Luna Park.

www.lunapark.com

QUEENS

Flushing Meadows Carousel: Cobbled together from two old Coney Island carousels for the 1964-65 World's Fair, it features mostly horses, one lion, and two chariots.

Fantasy Forest Amusement Park Corona Park,
www.nycgovparks.org

ROLL ON THE RIVER
WITH FREE KAYAKING

Few things compare with seeing NYC from the water, which is easy to do thanks to several nonprofit groups that loan out free, candy-colored, one-person and two-person kayaks to paddle around on the Hudson and East rivers between Memorial Day and Columbus Day. The largest concession is Downtown Boathouse out of Pier 26 on the Hudson, with another location on Pier 101 on Governors Island. Kayaking is limited to thirty- or forty-five-minute slots, so you can't wander far enough to get into the path of a multi-thousand-passenger cruise ship or other river traffic. Just sign a waiver, don a life jacket, and grab a paddle. It's a popular activity on hot summer weekend days, and because there are no reservations, be prepared to wait your turn.

www.downtownboathouse.org
www.manhattancommunityboathouse.org
www.northbrooklynboatclub.org
www.licboathouse.org

RUN AROUND
AT THE NYC MARATHON

Run through all five NYC boroughs, starting on the Staten Island side of the Verrazano-Narrows Bridge and ending in Central Park, after a circuitous route through Brooklyn, the Bronx, and Queens. Unlike other top marathons that require prior marathon experience, NYC rules allow almost anybody eighteen years or older with a heartbeat to run, which means there can be a half dozen applicants for each of the 51,000 slots. So unless you are classified as an "elite" or accredited runner who is guaranteed entry, your name is thrown into the lottery hat with no guarantee of winning a coveted bib. The NYC Marathon has been held annually since 1970, usually the first weekend in November. The records to beat are 2:05:06 by Geoffrey Mutai (men, 2011) and 2:22:31 by Margaret Okayo (women, 2003).

www.tcsnycmarathon.org

ALTERNATIVE #1
New York Road Runners Midnight Run in Central Park on New Year's Eve, www.nyrr.org

ALTERNATIVE #2
The Five Boro Bike Tour held every May, www.bikenewyork.org

GET HOOKED
WITH SHEEPSHEAD BAY FISHING BOATS

Depending on the season, it's fluke, flounder, porgies, sea bass, or huge bluefish, and sometimes more than one variety at a time. Take your pick of a half-dozen fishing boats with names such as *Captain Dave*, *Ocean Eagle V*, *Marilyn Jean IV,* and *Ranger VI*, all outfitted with modern fish-finding sonar so you don't return empty handed. Passengers range from salty regulars to first-timers. Crews help squeamish passengers bait their hooks or unhook the caught fish, and they even offer recipes for cooking your catch. Day trips and night excursions take you three to five miles into the Atlantic. Boats go out year-round, weather permitting, and return to docks usually lined with folks waiting to buy the freshest fish in town.

Docks along Emmons Ave. between E. 21st and 28th streets, Brooklyn

TIP

Chow down on chowders, seafood, and pastas at Randazzo's Clam Bar, 2017 Emmons Avenue at 21st Street, which is still family-run since opening in 1932.

www.randazzosclambar.nyc

ENJOY THE ONE AND ONLY
CONEY ISLAND

Okay, so it's lost some of its luster since the first half of the last century, when it was a world-class summer escape for millions of New Yorkers in the days before air conditioning. The wide white-sand Atlantic Ocean beach and pounding surf haven't changed, nor has that first heart-stopping drop on the Cyclone wooden roller coaster. You can still hear the satisfying "snap" of the hot dog casings at Nathan's Famous, where that famous hot-dog-eating contest is held on July Fourth, and the wide Boardwalk still beckons for strolling or people watching. Try to win a stuffed animal from the carnival-style games of chance, stay out of the path of a demonic driver on the bumper car rides, and be amazed at old-fashioned sword swallowers and other circus acts at the Coney Island Circus Sideshow. Don't forget to pack some wet wipes to get yourself un-sticky after wrestling with fresh-spun cotton candy.

www.coneyisland.com

LOVE IT
AT THE US OPEN

The last Grand Slam event of the year is held at the largest tennis venue in the world, a facility with thirty-two courts and a 22,547-seat stadium, named for tennis icons and pioneers who broke gender and racial barriers. The USTA Billie Jean King National Tennis Center and the Arthur Ashe Stadium have been the scene of some epic battles, including Pete Sampras besting Andre Agassi and Venus Williams defeating sister Serena, both in 2001; Novak Djokovic upsetting Roger Federer in 2010; and Rafael Nadal recovering enough from a 2016 wrist injury to win his sixteenth Grand Slam title in 2017. But you don't have to mortgage the house or car for a ticket to watch the big names serve it up. Tickets for qualifying matches are cheaper and easier to get, and you'll still learn something watching these future superstars play. The US Open is easy to get to: take the #7 to the same stop as you would for baseball's New York Mets. That would be the Mets-Willets Point station.

www.usopen.org

WALK ACROSS
THE BROOKLYN BRIDGE

When engineer John Augustus Roebling designed and built the suspension bridge linking Manhattan and Brooklyn across the East River in 1870, it made international headlines as an architectural marvel. It also changed NYC forever by kickstarting Brooklyn from a rural backwater to an integral part of a dynamic and growing city. More than two dozen men died building it, including Roebling, whose wife, Emily, finished the job. Interesting fact: They met when he was searching for the perfect limestone north of NYC in the Hudson Valley and stayed at her parents' inn. The Brooklyn Bridge is a NYC icon, and thousands walk or bicycle over it daily, for exercise or as part of their workday commute. The view of New York Harbor from the walkways elevated above the automotive level is stunning any time of day, but especially at sunset from the Brooklyn side, when Lower Manhattan's glass skyscrapers literally glow. So have a camera handy.

From Manhattan, enter the bridge from Centre Street east of City Hall.
www.nyc.gov

TIP
There's a metal grid walkway, so shoes with covered toes are recommended (and no high heels, ladies).

SET THE TREND
ON THE HIGH LINE

From 1934 to 1980, this 1.45-mile elevated track delivered railroad cars full of hogs, sides of beef, and crates of chickens to what was then the seedy, gritty Meatpacking District, which supplied the city's food stores and restaurants. It fell into disuse, was abandoned, and was due to be torn down in 1999. A small group of local visionaries fought to save it and turn it into a park, and they were successful beyond their wildest dreams. The High Line now attracts some five million visitors a year and has inspired a worldwide "rails to trails" movement to repurpose other abandoned tracks into walkways and bikeways. It also turned the old warehouse neighborhood into fashionable Meapo, with designer boutiques, trendy restaurants, art galleries, and new "star-chitecture" hotels and apartment buildings. Even the Whitney Museum of American Art moved here. But the beautifully landscaped park is a victim of its own success. With some sections just six to eight feet wide, it's often gridlocked, and, with entrance and exit staircases several blocks apart, it can feel claustrophobic at times. Avoid the thickest crowds by visiting on weekdays.

The High Line runs from Gansevoort St. (just below 14th St.) to W. 34th St. 212-500-6035, www.thehighline.org

PUCK AROUND
AT ROYAL PALMS SHUFFLEBOARD CLUB

The city's first and only shuffleboard venue is a brightly lit, 17,000-square-foot space with a Palm Beach-inspired theme, including two tropical bars. There are ten regulation shuffleboard courts, and it's popular enough that players are limited to one hour per court to give the next group a shot. There are bingo nights, league nights, a DJ, and instruction for never-evers who thought shuffleboard was only for senior citizens. RPSC is open until midnight on weekdays and until 2 a.m. on weekends. Nobody under twenty-one is admitted at any time.

514 Union St., Gowanus, Brooklyn, 347-223-4410
www.royalpalmsbrooklyn.com

SKATE
AT WOLLMAN RINK

Opened in 1949 at the southern edge of Central Park and named for the philanthropist who funded it, Wollman Rink doesn't have the touristy appeal of skating in Rockefeller Center—or its sky-high prices. Surrounded by skyscrapers that glitter at night and sparkle during the day, skating here is always magical, especially when the park is dusted with snow. Must be why Wollman is so popular for date night. The rink is large enough for the middle section to offer room to figure skaters practicing acrobatic spins and jumps. When the ice melts, Wollman turns into a Victorian-style amusement park with kiddie-sized rides.

www.centralpark.com

ALTERNATIVES

Equally large **Lasker Rink** is at the northern edge of Central Park and is also named for a benefactor. It turns into a public outdoor swimming pool in season.

The **Rink at Bryant Park** is part of the annual Winter Village. Skating is free, but not rentals.

www.bryantpark.org

The indoor **Sky Rink at Chelsea Piers** is open year-round, but public sessions at the twin rinks are squeezed in between hockey leagues, figure-skating shows, and filming TV commercials.

23rd St. and the Hudson River
www.chelseapiers.com

PLAY BALL
WITH THE A-TEAMS

The Brooklyn Cyclones are the minor-league feeder team for the New York Mets, and the Staten Island Yankees perform the same service for the Bronx Bombers. Both A-teams play in small, family-friendly stadiums, where you can be up close and personal to the action from any seat, and the best ticket in the house is under $20. The Cyclones play at MCU Park, home-run distance from the Coney Island Boardwalk, and the "Baby Bombers" bat it out in a stadium that is a few minutes' walk from the St. George ferry landing.

www.brooklyncyclones.com
www.milb.com/staten-island

GIVE A SALUTE
TO GOVERNORS ISLAND

Two hundred years of military history at Governors Island, including as a US Army and later US Coast Guard base, ended in the 1990s when the uniforms left this island in the New York harbor and its 172 acres became a car-free national park. The old Colonels Row barracks and officers' buildings are used for art displays and workshops, and there's a huge manmade section called The Hills, with a granite climbing scramble for adults and slides for kids, and spectacular skyline views from just about any point. One of the most popular events on the island's busy calendar is the Jazz Age Lawn Party, on the old Parade Grounds, with attendees dressed in their *Great Gatsby* best. Access to the historic playground is via ferries from both Brooklyn and Manhattan.

www.govisland.com

TAKE A HIKE
WITH SHOREWALKERS

The motto of this all-volunteer group is "Seeing the world at three miles per hour." These are guided walks, some longer than others, along NYC's waterfront parks, across bridges, and around lakes. Shorewalkers also goes beyond the borders of NYC, to similar waterside walks in the Hudson Valley and New Jersey. There are walks just about every weekend year-round, and any one you choose to join has the same price—$3—which supports the Shorewalkers' programs to protect, preserve, and promote the city's shores.

www.shorewalkers.org

DO THE DE-FIN-ITIVE EXPERIENCE
AT THE NEW YORK AQUARIUM

It's Shark Week year-round here. The aquarium showcases several varieties of these formidable fish, as well as the less spine-chilling seahorses, turtles, rays, and other marine life. The Coney Island outpost of the Wildlife Conservation Society sustained massive damage from Hurricane Sandy in 2012, requiring a whopping $158 million rebuild that took nearly six years to complete. It's bigger and better than before, including the Ocean Wonders: Sharks! exhibit in a building of its own that lets you get eyeball-to-eyeball with the fearsome creatures. Interactive displays explain the perils of over-fishing, the effects of climate change on marine life, and the importance of saving endangered species and coral reefs. When you're done, one of the most famous Atlantic Ocean beaches in the world is just down the block, and the Cyclone—one of the most famous roller coasters on the planet—is just a five-minute walk away.

602 Surf Ave.
www.nyaquarium.com

GET OUT ON THE TOWN
DURING NYC FLEET WEEK

Every Memorial Day week, as many as a dozen active ships disgorge 3,500 or more US Navy sailors, US Marines, and US Coast Guard service members in the real-life version of the iconic Hollywood musical *On the Town,* written by New Yorkers Leonard Bernstein, Betty Comden, and Adolph Green and choreographed by Jerome Robbins. You know the words from its most famous song—"New York, New York! It's a helluva town. / The Bronx is up, but the Battery's down. / The people ride in a hole in the ground"—sung and danced by Frank Sinatra, Gene Kelly, and Jules Munshin. When not on shore leave, the real military men and women are aboard, demonstrating and explaining the latest hardware and equipment to wide-eyed civilian visitors, and entertaining tourists with military band concerts in Times Square. NYC Fleet Week always begins with a Parade of Ships past the Statue of Liberty and the site of the 9/11 attack on the World Trade Center, with all hands on deck and saluting.

militarynews.com/app/fleetweeknewyork

TIP
The Intrepid Sea, Air & Space Museum, which plays a central role in NYC Fleet Week, is open year-round, offering the opportunity to explore the space shuttle Enterprise. Scotty, beam me up.

Credit: US Navy Mass Communication Specialist 1st Class Julie Matyascik/ Released

CULTURE AND HISTORY

SEE THE LADY IN THE HARBOR:
THE STATUE OF LIBERTY

There are two ways to get a close-up of the world's most famous woman: You can admire her from aboard the Staten Island Ferry (free) or from one of the many sightseeing boats (ticketed) that ply New York Harbor. Or, you can actually walk around Liberty Island, named for its famous resident, and get into the base of the statue that was an 1884 gift from the people of France. Interesting fact: Money for the pedestal was raised through a Victorian version of Kickstarter launched by NYC newspaper publisher Joseph Pulitzer. The advantage of being one of the poor, tired, huddled masses visiting Lady Liberty is that your ticket includes neighboring Ellis Island, where something like one million immigrants were processed in the early 1900s, including perhaps your own ancestors. Both the Statue of Liberty and Ellis Island have excellent museums, and because both are National Park Service sites there are free tours by park rangers.

National Park Service
www.nps.gov

ALTERNATIVE
Circle Line, Pier 83 at W. 43rd St., 212-563-3200
www.circleline42.com

TIPS

Statue Cruises is the only service licensed to dock at either island. Purchase tickets online to avoid waiting in line to buy them in Battery Park.

www.statuecruises.com

Visit the Statue of Liberty first to give yourself time later for tracing your American roots in the comprehensive database on Ellis Island.

FUN FACTS

Lady Liberty is 305 feet, one inch tall, from the ground to the tip of the torch—the height of a twenty-two-story building—and was the tallest structure in NYC at her debut.

MOURN
AT THE NATIONAL SEPTEMBER 11 MEMORIAL AND MUSEUM

At the National September 11 Memorial and Museum, docents and guards are specially trained to spot an impending emotional collapse and carry tissues for those who merely cry. This compelling exhibit is underground, in the very guts of the World Trade Center complex. Thousands of artifacts are displayed, from a huge fire truck melted out of shape by the searing heat to melted IDs of WTC office workers and the dust-covered shoes of a newspaper photographer covering the story of the day that changed us all forever. Photos and videos pay homage to each of the 2,973 victims, including heartbreaking messages to loved ones from those stuck inside the Twin Towers and on the hijacked planes, and video clips of survivors' stories and those of first responders. The 9/11 museum is open daily, except on 9/11 when it is closed to the public for the annual ceremony for families and first responders, including the hundreds of NYPD, NYFD, and Port Authority police who have died since of cancer and respiratory illnesses from working "The Pile" searching for remains in the sad days and weeks after 9/11.

1 Albany St., corner of Greenwich St., 212-266-5211
www.911memorial.org

9/11 MEMORIAL

While tickets are required for the museum, the memorial plaza is free. Officially known as *Reflections of Absence*, two thirty-foot-deep waterfalls, the largest manmade waterfalls in the United States, outline the footprint of each of the Twin Towers. The perpetually falling water signifies our unending tears, and the empty center signifies the void in our hearts. Names of all the victims are engraved in marble panels bordering the waterfalls, and docents with tablets help visitors find a particular name, hometown, or country (more than three hundred foreign nationals from eighty-four countries died in the attacks). More than four hundred trees have been planted in the plaza area, creating a shaded park also popular as a lunch spot for local office workers. Look for the so-called Miracle Tree, which survived the terrorist attack and still grows, becoming a symbol of regeneration and hope.

MUSEUM STORE

Unfortunately, cheap counterfeit goods are being sold by street vendors, so be sure to shop for official, licensed 9/11 products, which include NYPD and NYFD logo merchandise, at the museum store, knowing that your purchase price supports the museum.

Museum stores at 180 Greenwich St.,
as well as inside museum

SAY THANK YOU, MR. PRESIDENT
AT FEDERAL HALL

George Washington took the oath of office here in 1789 to become the first US president, back when NYC was the nation's capital. A larger-than-life statue of him dominates the steps outside the site, which became a national memorial in 1955. The small museum focuses on the tumultuous beginnings of the United States. National Park Service rangers give free guided tours, and there are events featuring Revolutionary War re-enactors.

26 Wall St.
www.nps.gov

TIP
Before taking the oath of office, Gen. Washington had a going-away dinner with his officers at Fraunces Tavern, a few blocks away, which has been operating since 1762. In addition to a menu of Colonial-style food and drink downstairs, there's a museum upstairs.

54 Pearl St., 212-968-1776
www.frauncestavern.com

SHOW ME THE MONEY
AT THE FEDERAL RESERVE BANK

You'll feel like a million here. As much as $100 billion is stored here, in a combo of gleaming gold bars and crisp paper bills, stacked to the ceiling in a seriously reinforced vault five stories underground. There are free daily tours, except on weekends and bank holidays, which include a short film on how bank employees process and protect all that money. Tours must be requested in advance (no walk-ins). Expect heightened security to enter, and don't expect to take any photos—secure lockers are provided for bags and anything that could snap a photo.

33 Liberty St., 212-720-6130
www.newyorkfed.org

GO DUTCH
AT THE DYCKMAN
FARMHOUSE MUSEUM

The Dyckman family farmed this part of Northern Manhattan for two centuries, beginning in the 1600s. This stone and clapboard house is the last remaining Revolutionary Era farmhouse in Manhattan. It is filled with historic artifacts, including uniforms worn by the Hessian mercenaries who camped out here when the patriot Dyckmans fled north to relatives in the Hudson Valley. There's a lush, quiet garden behind the house, which fronts on busy Broadway.

4881 Broadway at 204th St., 212-304-9422
www.dyckmanfarmhouse.org

TIP

Make a day of it and visit Inwood Hill Park, a few blocks north at the northernmost tip of Manhattan. This is where Peter Minuit is said to have purchased the island in 1626 from the local Lenape tribe for $24 worth of trinkets and beads. The park has Manhattan's only salt marsh, dotted with mallards and other water birds, and the last remaining untouched forest in NYC, along with ballfields, shaded paths, and knockout views across the Hudson River.

SEE SMALL SCREENS AND BIG STARS
AT THE PALEY CENTER FOR MEDIA

Founded by William S. Paley, who also founded CBS, this museum of broadcasting examines how media and society reflect and influence each other. You could spend a month here watching or listening to a treasure trove of historical archives of news and sports programs, sitcoms and dramas, music and dance performances, and more, from 1920s radio broadcasts to '50s TV pioneers such as Milton Berle to last weekend's *SNL*. Special screenings include appearances by the actors. There's also a free gallery of TV-based gaming, such as Xbox, which does not require museum admission.

25 W. 52nd St., 212-621-6600
www.paleycenter.org

TIP
Adjacent to the museum is Paley Park, the first of NYC's so-called "vest pocket" parks. Built on the footprint of a former small building, the park has chairs and tables and a soothing waterfall wall that blocks out street noise.

GET A TWO-FER:
THE BROOKLYN MUSEUM AND BOTANIC GARDEN

It's a shame the Brooklyn Museum is overshadowed by the Met, because they are both world-class museums. Brooklyn's is the second-largest art museum in the city, also with a knock-out Egyptian wing, an American painting wing with artists including Georgia O'Keeffe, and must-see special exhibits such as the recent David Bowie show that included his personal archives. The adjoining Brooklyn Botanic Garden is an ethereal spot with a Japanese garden pond and *tonsu*, and a Celebrity Path celebrating such famous Brooklynites as Rita Hayworth, Barbra Streisand, Mel Brooks, and Mae West. The Eastern Parkway subway stop is at the front door of both.

www.brooklynmuseum.org
www.bbg.org

EXPLORE A MILLIONAIRE MANSION
AT WAVE HILL

Built in 1843 as a country getaway house by a wealthy descendant of one of the signers of the Declaration of Independence, this hilltop mansion was later rented by such famous residents as Mark Twain, Arturo Toscanini, and Teddy Roosevelt. Luckily, the family of the next buyer, a millionaire banker, donated it to the city in the 1960s. The gardens and lawns overlooking the Hudson River and granite-faced Palisade cliffs are spectacular, the winding paths and pergolas have a Victorian feel, and the greenhouse is an oasis of tropical succulents. Family-friendly programs include beekeeping and gardening, and there are rotating art exhibits.

W. 249th St. and Independence Ave., Bronx, 718-549-3200
www.wavehill.org

GET TO THE TOP OF THE ROCK
AT ROCKEFELLER CENTER

John D. Rockefeller built Rockefeller Center, a sprawling post-Depression urban-renewal complex of nineteen commercial buildings, the tallest and most famous of which is 30 Rockefeller Plaza, home of NBC. Of course, the Studio Tour is a must, as is the Top of the Rock observation deck, with sweeping 360-degree views that include the Empire State Building and new World Trade Center to the south and George Washington Bridge and the Cloisters to the north. Or, get the same view without the crowds at Bar SixtyFive, on the sixty-fifth floor, for the price of a cocktail. Be sure to get a self-guided map for the massive museum-quality Diego Rivera murals ringing the 30 Rock lobby that depict the role of the working man in the industrial world.

www.rockefellercenter.com

ALTERNATIVE

The eight-story Vessel centerpiece of the new Hudson Yards mini-city looks like an inverted beehive. Climb the stairs or take the tiny elevator for knock-out views from any of several dozen balcony viewpoints. Bonus: it's free.

Hudson Yards, 11th Ave. at 34th St,
www.hudsonyardsnewyork.com

HEAR AMERICAN STORIES
AT IMMIGRANT MUSEUMS

New York is a city of immigrants, so it shouldn't be surprising that there are museums about the immigrant experience. These two are on the Lower East Side, the first stop for millions seeking a better life in America.

Tenement Museum: Climb the creaky stairs to cramped, airless rooms and a bathroom shared with your neighbors, and you'll understand instantly why immigrants worked practically twenty-four/seven to afford to move to better neighborhoods. The apartments of the Moore, Gumpertz, Levine, and Baldizzi families, who lived here between the 1860s and 1930s, combine their actual possessions and real, faded, and peeling wallpaper for a timeless story of hardship and hope. This is the reality, far more gritty than Hollywood versions.

103 Orchard St., 212-982-8420
www.tenement.org

Museum of Chinese in America (MOCA): From slippers for binding feet and axes used to build the railroad that linked the East and West coasts to exhibits featuring today's tech-preneurs and star chefs, MOCA tells of the Chinese immigrant experience. After decades in a dimly lit tenement in Chinatown, MOCA moved into a bright new building next door by Maya Lin, who also designed the Vietnam Veterans Memorial in Washington, DC. Rotating exhibits showcase a single artist or style, such as calligraphy, the history of a single family through generations of photos, or the social importance of a single game, such as mah-jongg.

215 Centre St. between Howard and Grand, 212-619-4785
www.mocanyc.org/visit

EXPERIENCE NATIVE PRIDE
AT THE NATIONAL MUSEUM
OF THE AMERICAN INDIAN

All the native peoples of North and South America are represented here, from the Inuit of the Arctic Circle to the Taíno of the Caribbean and the tribes of Tierra Del Fuego and Patagonia, along with artifacts from many US tribes. Rotating exhibits range from contemporary art and fashion by Native Americans to the role of women in native cultures. There's a juried market each holiday season of hand-crafted jewelry, basketry, and other gift items by top US tribal artists. NMAI is a branch of the Smithsonian, with always-free admission. The building itself is a Beaux Arts gem, listed on the National Register of Historic Places, whose official name is the Alexander Hamilton US Custom House. It was designed by Cass Gilbert, the most renowned architect of the time, with a spectacular central rotunda and dome reminiscent of the US Capitol in Washington, DC. There are federal government offices upstairs, including an office of US Customs and Border Protection, where you can apply for Trusted Traveler designations to speed your way through airport security lines.

1 Bowling Green, 212-514-3700
nmai.si.edu/visit/newyork

● ●

IMPROVE YOUR KARMA
AT THE JACQUES MARCHAIS
MUSEUM OF TIBETAN ART

Built in 1945 to resemble a Tibetan temple by art dealer and Asian art collector Jacques Marchais, this little gem is overshadowed by homes built more recently in the style of Tony Soprano. It's an oasis with silk brocade pillows on benches, so you are comfy while admiring Buddha statues, mandalas, and more from Tibet, Nepal, and Bhutan, some dating back to the sixteenth century. The Dalai Lama has visited, but as far as we know did not participate in the meditation workshops or yoga classes.

338 Lighthouse Ave., Staten Island, 718-987-3500
www.tibetanmuseum.org

Take the S74 bus from Staten Island Ferry's St. George Terminal
to the Lighthouse Avenue stop, and walk up the hill
(five to ten minutes) to the museum.

ALTERNATIVE
Get more good karma at the Rubin Museum of Art, which grew out of another collector's love of historic Himalayan and Indian art, including fabrics. The Rubin also has rotating exhibits featuring contemporary Asian artists and designers.

150 W. 17th St., 212-620-5000
www.rubinmuseum.org

REFLECT ON SLAVERY'S HISTORY
AT THE AFRICAN BURIAL GROUND NATIONAL MONUMENT

In 1991, construction workers excavating for a new skyscraper in the Financial District discovered the remains of some fifteen thousand skeletons buried here in the 1600s and 1700s, all of them slaves or freed slaves, stacked in layers in unmarked graves. The remains were re-interred at Howard University, and the plot of ground then known as the Negroes Burial Ground became the African Burial Ground National Monument. It's a tranquil site, as befits a cemetery, even one in the middle of a busy city, except during Kwanzaa when there are ongoing events here. A striking black marble semicircle is etched with African symbols, and marble benches and a small waterfall invite introspection and relaxation.

Southwest corner of Elk and Duane streets, 212-637-2019,
plus an interpretive center at 290 Broadway
www.nps.gov/afbg

GIRD YOUR LOINS
AT THE CLOISTERS

John D. Rockefeller built this marvel to house his impressive collection of Roman and medieval art. Some of the world's oldest tapestries, from the fifteenth and sixteenth centuries, are here, including the gems known as the Unicorn Tapestries. Gardens bloom with herbs and plants from the Middle Ages, including one dedicated to those pictured in the tapestries, and a reliquary gleams with gold and silver religious objects. In warmer months there are concerts of medieval music and even jousting tournaments. The monastery-like setting was assembled, like a jigsaw puzzle, from parts of medieval French and Spanish cloisters and chapels, atop the highest point in Manhattan in Ft. Tryon Park. The Cloisters is part of the Metropolitan Museum of Art, better known as "The Met," and admission to one includes same-day admission to the other.

99 Margaret Corbin Dr., 212-923-3700
www.metmuseum.org

WHERE TO SEE HAMILTON

Can't get, or afford, a ticket to the hit Broadway musical? No worries. See the inspiration here.

Trinity Churchyard: Alexander Hamilton is buried here with his wife, Eliza, and their eldest son, Philip, along with other Revolutionary Era leaders, including John Peter Zenger, the newspaper publisher whose libel trial helped establish the right of a free press. The multi-tasking Hamilton was himself a newspaper publisher; he founded the *New York Evening Post* in 1801, still publishing today as the *New York Post*.

74 Trinity Place
www.trinitywallstreet.org

Hamilton Grange National Monument: Hamilton built this Federal-style house in 1801 when the hilltop area now called Hamilton Heights was still farmland. It was his principal residence when he was killed in 1804 in a duel with Aaron Burr. Park rangers give free tours.

Convent Ave. at 141st St., 212-283-5154
www.nps.gov

Morris-Jumel Mansion: Built in 1765 by Roger Morris, also as a country getaway. George Washington camped out here briefly during the Revolutionary War and later held the first presidential cabinet meeting here, which included both Hamilton and Burr. In one of those historic twists of fate, the house was purchased by merchant Stephen Jumel, whose widow Eliza married Burr in the front parlor. Lin-Manuel Miranda wrote parts of the mega-hit musical here.

65 Jumel Terrace at 160th St., 212-923-8008
www.morrisjumel.org

Statues: Find Hamilton standing tall at the entrance to Central Park's East Drive, at 83rd Street and Fifth Avenue, in front of Hamilton Hall at Columbia University, his alma mater, then known as King's College. See another likeness at St. Luke's Episcopal Church in Hamilton Heights, where he worshipped.

PEEK AT PRICELESS BOOKS
AT THE MORGAN LIBRARY AND MUSEUM

Millionaire banker J. P. Morgan famously said, in answer to a question about his yacht, "If you have to ask how much it costs, you can't afford it." So we won't ask how much it cost to buy the Gutenberg Bible on display here, or any of the thousands of first editions and other leather-bound treasures that fill shelves stacked three stories high. Lucky for us, Morgan's private library and office are now public, connected by a marble lobby. There are also rotating exhibits of literary significance, including personal letters and other artifacts, ranging from such serious topics as Martin Luther and the Reformation to more whimsical ones, such as showcasing Maurice Sendak and his iconic children's book *Where the Wild Things Are*.

225 Madison Ave. at 37th St.
www.themorgan.org

ALTERNATIVE

Henry Clay Frick was another Gilded Age millionaire, via Pittsburgh steel (he was one of the founders of U. S. Steel). Also lucky for us, he bequeathed his Fifth Ave. mansion to display his outstanding medieval and Renaissance art collection.

The Frick Collection, 1 E. 70th St.
www.frick.org

JUST VISIT
THE GREEN-WOOD CEMETERY

One of the few US cemeteries with National Historic Landmark status, Brooklyn's Green-Wood has an outstanding collection of architecturally significant statues and mausoleums, some dating to the 1830s when it opened. Many world-famous New Yorkers are among the 560,000 permanent residents, including stained-glass king Louis Comfort Tiffany, composer Leonard Bernstein, and Charles Ebbets, owner of the beloved Brooklyn Dodgers, who played in Ebbets Field before taking the advice of newspaperman Horace Greeley, also buried here, to "go west, young man." There's a section of graves of Civil War soldiers, and the park-like setting of winding paths, glacial lakes, and mature trees attracts birdwatchers along with history and art enthusiasts. Hop on a trolley tour, including one to Revolutionary War-related sites, or attend concerts and other events, such as a Victorian-style circus.

By subway: Take the R train to the 25th St. Station;
walk one block east to the main entrance.

5th Ave. and 25th St., 718-210-3080
www.green-wood.com

SAY AMEN
AT THE CATHEDRAL CHURCH OF ST. JOHN THE DIVINE

You could find solace and respite in any one of NYC's world-class cathedrals, or you could seek more. At the largest Anglican church in the world, there are daily guided tours of the art and architectural highlights, and "vertical tours" in which you climb a spiral staircase for a close-up view of the magnificent stained-glass windows and a picture-postcard view of the city from a buttress. There's also a popular Halloween "crypt crawl" and the even more popular annual New Year's Eve Concert for Peace.

1047 Amsterdam Ave. at 112th St., 212-316-7540
www.stjohndivine.org

ALTERNATIVE

Tours of St. Patrick's Cathedral, at 50th Street and Fifth Avenue are self-guided with the church's free smartphone app. Leave a small donation to help pay for the recent $180 million restoration of this NYC landmark, which opened in 1879.

212-753-2261
www.saintpatrickscathedral.org

STOP TRAFFIC
DURING MANHATTANHENGE

Twice a year, the sun lines up directly with Manhattan's east-west street grid, and the setting sun lights up both the north and south sides of the street. The designation "Manhattanhenge" was coined by Neil deGrasse Tyson, the Hayden Planetarium's rock-star astrophysicist, as a wordplay on Stonehenge, in England, where the sun aligns with the ancient stones on the sunrise of the summer solstice with similarly dramatic effect. The best place to see this unique urban solar display in mid-May and again in mid-July (exact dates change annually) is on the 42nd Street overpass by the United Nations. Because it's tough to squeeze in between all the serious photographers with tripods and long lenses, join the cellphone crowd in Times Square flooding onto the roadway and literally stopping traffic.

ALTERNATIVE

At the Hayden Planetarium, adjoining the American Museum of Natural History, astrophysicists explain the astronomy behind the spectacle, then take you to an overlook for a memorable view.

81 Central Park West at 81st St., 212-769-5100
www.haydenplanetarium.org

SHOUT "LAND, HO!"
AT THE LITTLE RED LIGHTHOUSE

What, you never heard of Jeffrey's Hook Lighthouse? That's the original name, but it's been known as the Little Red Lighthouse ever since the debut of Hildegarde H. Swift's still-popular 1942 children's book, *The Little Red Lighthouse and the Great Gray Bridge*. It's Manhattan's last remaining lighthouse, no longer operational thanks to the great gray George Washington Bridge overhead, but the waterside views south to the Manhattan skyline and west and north across the Hudson River are spectacular. The Urban Park Rangers give regular tours (free) between spring and fall.

Fort Washington Park, Riverside Dr. at W. 178th St., 212-304-2365
www.historichousetrust.org

TIP
Check out the National Lighthouse Museum, in a 1912 building steps from the Staten Island landing of the Staten Island Ferry, for the history and value of these important structures, which were replaced by modern GPS technology.

200 The Promenade at Lighthouse Point
www.lighthousemuseum.org

TAKE THE AERIAL TRAM
TO ROOSEVELT ISLAND

NYC's only aerial tram links the east side of Manhattan with Roosevelt Island, in the middle of the East River. It's a 147-acre island with middle-income housing, a high-tech Cornell University campus, and waterside promenades with magnificent skyline views. Walk or take the free shuttle to Four Freedoms Park, at the island's southern tip, a memorial to FDR and his famous WWII speech about the fight for freedom of speech and worship, and freedom from want and fear. You could also take the subway to Roosevelt Island, but the tram is so much more memorable.

1 FDR Four Freedoms Park, 212-204-8831
www.fdrfourfreedomspark.org

LOOK UP
AT THE SKYSCRAPER MUSEUM

Even though New York City didn't invent the skyscraper, it is home to several of the world's most famous ones. The Woolworth Building, the Chrysler Building, and the Empire State Building all were the tallest in the world at the time of their construction, as were the World Trade Center Twin Towers. So it should not be surprising to find a museum dedicated to the world's tall, taller, and tallest architecture, skylines, and the cultural influences that shaped them.

39 Battery Place, 212-945-6324
www.skyscraper.org

ALTERNATIVE
Directly across the street is the Museum of Jewish Heritage/A Living Memorial to the Holocaust. Exhibits combine the horror of the past, including eyewitness stories about resistance and faith, and programs on the dangers of intolerance around the world. A contemplative outdoor garden fittingly overlooks the Statue of Liberty.

6 Battery Place, 646-437-4200
www.mjhnyc.org

DESIGN A FASHIONABLE EXPERIENCE
AT THE MUSEUM AT FIT

The Fashion Institute of Technology (FIT) is the Harvard and Yale of fashion, and this two-floor museum is both a gem of historic fashions and a lab for future designers. Rotating exhibits focus on a theme, such as a particular designer, fabric, color, decade, or category, including shoes. FIT's footwear collection alone contains more than four thousand pairs of shoes, boots, sandals, and more. Or, maybe you prefer to flip through thousands of fashion photographs, including vintage issues of magazines such as *Vogue*. There's also a gallery showcasing student and faculty designs. Bonus: This is one of NYC's museums with free admission.

7th Ave. at 27th St., 212-217-4558
www.fitnyc.edu/museum

LEARN YOUR TIMES TABLES
AT THE NATIONAL MUSEUM OF MATH

If you think about it, everything from music and dance to computer codes, the architecture of the buildings we live in, and the vehicles we drive is based on mathematics, and the whimsical exhibits here explore it all, entertaining and educating simultaneously. Ride a square-wheeled bicycle smoothly over a bumpy road, light up floor squares set up like a maze, figure out how a curved space is made up of only straight lines, drive on an unending Mobius strip, and more. Although most exhibits are designed for the grade-school and middle-school set, there are enough fun and games and technology to appeal to toddlers, teens, and adults. Affectionately known as MoMath, this is the only museum of its kind in the United States, which is odd because everything we see or do is based on math. It doesn't take an Einstein to figure that out.

11 E. 26th St., 212-542-0566
www.momath.org

GET ABOARD
THE HOLIDAY NOSTALGIA TRAIN

Travel back in time to when NYC subways had woven wicker seats, ceiling fans, and ceramic straps to hang onto, which gave riders the nickname "straphangers." Vintage trains that were in service between 1932 and 1977 are rolled out annually by the MTA for the five Sundays preceding New Year's Day. While the routes change slightly each year, what doesn't change is the nostalgic appeal of riding a genuine vintage train for the same price as a modern ride.

www.nytransitmuseum.org

TIP
See more vintage "rolling stock," including buses, at the Transit Museum in Brooklyn. The annex inside Grand Central Terminal features a huge-- and free—display of vintage Lionel trains each holiday season, chugging along as many as eight separate tracks through a miniature NYC scene.

EXPLORE AN ARTISTIC STREET FAIR
AT THE MUSEUM MILE FESTIVAL

The one-mile section of Fifth Avenue between 82nd and 105th streets is polka-dotted with nearly a dozen of the world's most famous museums, including the Met and the Guggenheim; special interest museums, including the Jewish Museum, the Asia Society, and the Cooper Hewitt/Smithsonian Design Museum; and local faves such as the Museum of the City of New York and El Museo del Barrio. They give the stretch its name—Museum Mile—and each June it turns into a mile-long giant street party, with music, a kids' playground, food vendors, and free admission to all the museums.

www.museummilefestival.org

ALTERNATIVE
There's also a Night at the Museums in June, with similar free admission to the museums of Lower Manhattan, including the 9/11 Museum, and discounts at local restaurants.

www.nightatthemuseums.org

Credit: Beyond My Ken

SHOPPING AND FASHION

GET LOST IN THE STACKS
AT STRAND BOOKSTORE

With eighteen miles of shelves on three floors crammed with books, it's easy to get lost at Strand Bookstore. Fortunately there is a knowledgeable staff who can direct you to the section or to the specific book you want (employees must take a literacy test to work here). Strand has been buying and reselling used books and discounting recent best sellers since 1927. There are bargain bins in the front of the store and on the sidewalk outside, with prices starting at fifty cents, and a rare book room with prices into the multiple thousands for leather-bound first editions and books signed by famous historical figures.

828 Broadway at 12th St., 212-473-1452
www.strandbooks.com

TIP
One block away, Forbidden Planet NYC is one of the largest shops on the planet selling comic books, science fiction, and graphic novels, as well as the toys, collectibles, and superhero t-shirts their fans love.

832 Broadway, 212-473-1576
www.fpnyc.com

MORE INDIE AND SPECIALTY BOOKSTORES

Real paper books, for real page-turning, are alive and well at these other independent NYC bookstores:

McNally Jackson: With more than 100,000 titles in its literature selection alone, this is an important bookseller anywhere.

www.mcnallyjackson.com

Books of Wonder: Kids and the adults who love them love books enough to support two outposts of everything from *Goodnight Moon* to Harry Potter titles.

www.booksofwonder.com

Shakespeare & Co. has two locations in Manhattan, each with a unique 3D printer that will deliver books currently out of stock, or personal and family memoirs to share privately.

www.shakeandco.com

Rizzoli: For a zillion years, this Midtown bookstore has specialized in illustrated books and European magazines.

www.rizzolibookstore.com

Drama Book Shop: The number-one destination for books about film and theater, including plays, scripts, monologues, and in-store readings by actors and playwrights. Of course, it's in the Theater District.

www.dramabookshop.com

Kitchen Arts & Letters: Serving foodies more than thirteen thousand new, used, and out-of-print cookbooks, from soup to nuts.

www.kitchenartsandletters.com

Mysterious Bookshop: Agatha Christie and Ian Fleming would love this place, stocked floor-to-ceiling with crime, espionage, and suspense thrillers.

www.mysteriousbookshop.com

Kinokuniya: This NYC outpost of the Japanese chain offers groaning stacks of English-language new and used books and CDs at reasonable prices starting from $1.

www.kinokuniya.com

ENJOY THE OUTDOORS
AT PARAGON SPORTING GOODS

With the exception of golf and fishing paraphernalia, you can find anything you need for any sport legal in NYC in this sprawling, three-story store, plus repairs and the clothing and footwear to look good while doing them (or while you just make believe you're an athlete). It has tennis rackets and facilities for re-stringing them; skis, snowboards, and experts at tuning for both; and kayaks and paddles, sleeping bags and tents, backpacks small enough for grade school and large enough for hiking the Appalachian Trail, and GPS units to help you find your way home. There's an excellent children's department with team logo items. Paragon runs (pun intended) fitness training programs leading up to the New York City Marathon and bus trips to nearby ski and snowboard resorts in the Catskills and Vermont's Green Mountains in winter.

867 Broadway at 18th St., 212-255-8036
www.paragonsports.com

MEANDER ACROSS MILLIONAIRE'S ROW:
WEST FIFTY-SEVENTH STREET

The announcement in the early 2010s that a giant Nordstrom would open in a new residential building on west 57th Street helped turn the blocks between Eighth and Fifth avenues into "Millionaire's Row." There are now super-tall, super-luxurious condos and hotels and eager landlords blinded by dollar signs, who cashed in by driving out longtime tenants from older, lower-rise buildings. So the fashion retailer, with a separate Nordstrom for Men on Broadway between 57th and 58th streets, wound up sandwiched between a T. J. Maxx on 57th and Eighth Avenue and an upper-scale Bergdorf, Tiffany & Co., and Buccellati on the corners of 57th and Fifth, with Cartier, Louis Vuitton, and other prime designer names within a block or two.

www.nordstrom.com

SHOP DANISH MODERN
AT FLYING TIGER COPENHAGEN

An eclectic, even quirky, mix of colorful and well-designed items for adults and kids. There are storage bins and carry-alls, notebooks and notepads, kitchen and garden utensils, magnified "reader" glasses, animal-shaped pens and erasers, party favors, painting kits, puzzles, and more. Best of all, items range from $1 to $8. You have to search long and hard for anything more than $10, so you can afford to be impulsive. There are additional locations in the Flatiron, Upper East Side, Upper West Side, and Citypoint, Brooklyn.

www.flyingtiger.com

TIP

Check out these other discount chains for rock-bottom prices on merchandise that changes weekly.

Lot-Less Closeouts: Steep discounts on imported food items such as olive oil and chocolate, overstock clothing such as sports bras and sneakers, discontinued colors of name-brand cosmetics, housewares, etc.

www.lot-less.com

Jacks: This chain used to be called Jack's 99 Cent Stores, until prices went up to at least a buck. Bargain-priced groceries and brand-name household cleaners, clothing, office supplies, and even lightbulbs.

www.jacksnyc.com

HUNT FOR BARGAINS
AT CENTURY 21

This department store a few blocks from the Twin Towers of the World Trade Center was once one of NYC's best-kept secrets. Like much of downtown, that changed on 9/11, when images of its debris-covered racks of designer discount clothing, shoes, and accessories for both men and women were shown around the world. Since then, Century 21 has expanded into a chain, with a dozen locations in NYC and as far away as Florida. The original one downtown (22 Cortlandt Street) and another across from Lincoln Center (Broadway at 66th Street) attract mostly tourists, especially foreign visitors, scooping up everything from well-known brands of handbags and headphones to watches and wallets to sneakers and sweaters.

www.c21stores.com

BUILD IT
AT THE LEGO STORE

Budding young architects and engineers, and grownups with dexterous fingers and twenty/twenty eyesight, head here to browse and get hands-on playtime with bite-size plastic bits and figures. A feature everybody loves is the 3D animation kiosk, where planes and helicopters fly, and so on. Ditto the Lego Lounge in the back of the store, where kids can read Lego-themed books or play with colorful blocks while their caretakers recharge—literally—with comfy grown-up seating and outlets to power up fading electronics. There's another Lego Store in Rockefeller Center.

200 5th Ave. at 23rd St., 212-255-3217
www.lego.com

TIP

FAO Schwarz, founded in 1862, has re-opened with the largest toy store in town, to the delight of kids of all ages ready to play its life-sized piano—the one made famous in the movie *Big*—plus toys in sizes ranging from tiny to giraffe-sized, miniature trains, and more.

30 Rockefeller Plaza, 800-426-8697
www.faoschwarz.com

SNAG DESIGNER DISCOUNTS
AT 260 FIFTH SAMPLE SALE

The name is also the address and its merch, which is top designer clothing, shoes, handbags, and work-out gear at bottom-line discounts. Unlike T. J. Maxx or Marshall's, where multiple labels share a rack, this discounter offers just one or two labels for a few days at a time, followed by another designer, such as Lululemon, Rebecca Minkoff, or Diane von Furstenberg, looking to clear current and recent season overstock. Expect a rudimentary dressing room that's just a curtained-off communal space with not enough hooks or mirrors for the try-ons, but the upside is that your fellow fashionistas and bargainistas are more honest than a mirror for answering, "Does this make me look fat?"

260 5th Ave., 212-725-5400
www.260samplesale.com

HEAD TO CIRCUIT CITY:
THE B&H SUPERSTORE

The B&H Superstore is the largest store of its kind in NYC, and maybe the planet, for cameras and gear, computers and TVs, lighting and audio equipment, and other electronics you didn't know you needed, all at discount prices, along with the software, accessories, and carrying cases to make them happy and knowledgeable salespeople who know their brand or section intimately. So, while the gurus at the Nikon kiosk won't answer a question about Canon or Fuji, the ones at the laptop and tablet area here are equally adept at the pros and cons of PC vs. Mac. There are also regular free seminars and workshops to improve how you take or edit images, and free camera cleaning to get the dust off your sensors.

420 9th Ave. at 34th St., 212-444-6615
www.bandh.com

TIP
Adorama, at 21 West 17th Street, is smaller and less crowded, but with similar discount prices and also free seminars and workshops.

www.adorama.com

WEAR IT AGAIN, SAM
AT BUFFALO EXCHANGE

Whether you call it recycled, used, or previously worn, Buffalo Exchange provides a rotating collection of men's and women's clothing, shoes, and accessories, such as costume jewelry and ties, all in excellent condition. Mostly it carries sportswear and everyday staples such as jeans and shirts, but there are enough dress-for-success and cocktail outfits to make this destination shopping if you are looking for a bargain you'll wear just once. This is a nationwide chain, which means vast reselling/buying power, including brand-new manufacturer overstock. You can feel good about your bargain hunting because a portion of each re-sale supports an eco-friendly charity. There are five NYC locations: East Village and Chelsea in Manhattan, Williamsburg and Boerum Hill in Brooklyn, and Astoria in Queens.

www.buffaloexchange.com

EAT BREAKFAST
AT TIFFANY'S

Although Tiffany & Co. (the official name) has expanded around the world since its founding in 1837, nothing compares with the flagship at Fifth Avenue and 57th Street, where Audrey Hepburn so famously ate a muffin. Or was it a croissant? No matter. The historic five-story townhouse is filled with beautiful things that glitter, sparkle, and shine, from dazzling six-figure gemstone baubles in the glass cases on the main floor to a glazed plate upstairs for under $50 in the same Tiffany Blue color as its famous and equally stylish gift boxes. Tiffany became a recognized leader in the art and design of silver before founder Charles Lewis Tiffany began buying diamonds from the Kimberley mines in South Africa, and the rest, as they say, is history. Which includes Louis Comfort Tiffany, the founder's son, who branched out into gem-colored stained glass. You may have heard of his lamps and windows.

5th Ave. at 57th St., 212-755-8000
www.tiffany.com

STROLL ALONG
FIFTH AND MADISON AVENUES

Paris has the Champs-Élysées, Berlin has the Kurfurstendamm, and Los Angeles has Rodeo Drive. NYC, however, has two big shopping promenades: Fifth Avenue and Madison Avenue, two parallel rows of high-end designer shops and luxury residential buildings. Sadly, Fifth has gone seedy below 50th Street, taken over by tacky souvenir shops and even a medical marijuana dispensary. But between 50th and 59th streets you'll find top designer boutiques, and the only twenty-four/seven Apple Store in the city. After that, Fifth turns residential with Central Park on one side. The other is block after block of soaring apartment buildings and Gilded Age mansions, some of which have been turned into museums and foreign consulates, along with the Museum Mile that includes the Met and the Guggenheim. On parallel Madison Avenue, it's one high-fashion, high-priced designer boutique and jewelry store after another, from 50th Street to the 90s, like a two-mile-long mall for millionaires.

www.visit5thavenue.com

BET ON BARGAINS
AT PEARL RIVER MART

The city's largest Asian supermarket, at the border of Chinatown and Soho, features a vast array of items small and large: little silk purses, slippers, and scarves, and larger embroidered happy coats and jackets. Little bags of Asian snacks and teas, larger woks and steamers. Jars of spices and sauces in heat ranges from mild to "call the EMTs." Small party favors, large silk flowers, and bamboo furniture, plus handsome jade jewelry, an impressive array of chopsticks, from the plain wooden restaurant variety to intricate inlaid items worthy of putting in a display case, and all manner of plates and bowls, teapots and cups. Although most items are made in China, you'll also find goodies from neighbors Taiwan, Thailand, Vietnam, Cambodia, and Japan.

395 Broadway at Walker St. (Soho), 212-431-4770
www.pearlriver.com

INDULGE YOUR SWEET TOOTH
AT ECONOMY CANDY

This shop opened during the Depression to provide some sweetness to down-on-their-luck New Yorkers, and it is operated today by adult grandchildren of the founders. The specialty is old-fashioned candies at old-fashioned prices. This is where to find bags of Mary Janes and Tootsie Rolls, wax lips, jelly beans, M&M's in every color of the rainbow including teal and cream, Jordan almonds, Turkish taffy, and salt-water taffy. Economy Candy also stocks vintage lunch boxes and the largest selection of Pez dispensers on the planet. When was the last time you saw a package of C. Howard's violet-scented gum? There are also modern specialty candies, from M&M-like buttons imprinted with "It's a BOY" to rock candy swizzle sticks. Buy by the piece, package, or pound, from shelves and bins stacked to the ceiling. Just don't tell your dentist.

108 Rivington St. between Ludlow and Essex, 212-254-1531
www.economycandy.com

ATTEND AN AUCTION
AT CHRISTIE'S

Best known for its blockbuster auctions, such as the estate of Peggy and David Rockefeller in May 2018 that garnered more than $832 million for a treasure trove of Picassos, Renoirs, furniture, and baubles. Less well known is that these coveted collections are open to public viewing, free and with no appointment necessary, usually a week before the sale. It could be Old Masters or ancient hieroglyphs, rare printed books or fine jewelry, exhibited in spotlighted glass cases. The goods are on display weekdays in Christie's quietly elegant Rockefeller Center outpost, and because there's rarely anyone there it's like having your own small, private museum of masterpieces. All yours—for a few moments, at least.

20 Rockefeller Plaza (49th St. between 5th and 6th aves.)
212-636-2000
www.christies.com

TAKE YOUR MEDICINE
AT C. O. BIGELOW PHARMACY

This shop claims to be the oldest apothecary in America, in the same location since 1838. Originally, medications were compounded and dispensed by hand. Today, a modern high-tech robot fills prescriptions. This is also the place to find old-fashioned rose-scented salves and oils alongside modern make-up and bath products, herbal throat lozenges, and toothpaste from Italy. Just visiting the shop, with its wood paneling and shelves, is a soothing experience, as it was for such famous customers as Mark Twain and members of the Roosevelt family, who once lived nearby.

414 Sixth Ave., 212-533-2700
www.bigelowchemists.com

SUGGESTED
ITINERARIES

ONLY IN NEW YORK

Pass the Pickles at Katz's Delicatessen, 8

Enjoy the One and Only Coney Island, 66

Stop Traffic during Manhattanhenge, 105

Where to See Hamilton, 100

Join the Audience at Late-Night TV Shows, 46

See Where Stars Are Born at Apollo Theater, 50

Kick up a Storm at Radio City Music Hall, 36

See Broadway Stars at Sardi's, 14

HISTORY LESSONS

Hear American Stories at Immigrant Museums, 94

Reflect on Slavery's History at the African Burial Ground National
  Monument, 98

Go Dutch at the Dyckman Farmhouse Museum, 88

LOWER MANHATTAN IN A DAY

See the Lady in the Harbor: The Statue of Liberty, 82

Mourn at the National September 11 Memorial and Museum, 84

Experience Native Pride at the National Museum of the American Indian, 96

Say Thank You, Mr. President at Federal Hall, 86

Look Up at the Skyscraper Museum, 109

GREAT OUTDOORS

FAMILY FUN

ARTS AND CRAFTS

DATE NIGHT

SPORTY SPOTS

FOODIE FAVORITES

Credit: Leonard Zhukovsky / Shutterstock.com

ACTIVITIES
BY SEASON

SPRING

Be My Valentine at the Times Square Vow Renewal, 37

Get Out on the Town during NYC Fleet Week, 78

Explore an Artistic Street Fair at the Museum Mile Festival, 113

SUMMER

Grab a Partner at Midsummer Night Swing, 38

Roll on the River with Free Kayaking, 62

Stop Traffic during Manhattanhenge, 105

Shout "Land, Ho!" at the Little Red Lighthouse, 106

FALL

Run Around at the NYC Marathon, 63

Mangia at the Feast of San Gennaro, 24

See Superstars Perform at the Global Citizen Festival, 55

Don't Rain on My Parade: Balloonfest, 56

WINTER

Get Aboard the Holiday Nostalgia Train, 112

Kick up a Storm at Radio City Music Hall, 36

Skate at Wollman Rink, 72

Try Twenty-One Days of Prix Fixe: NYC Restaurant Week, 20

INDEX

Credit: kamikakazel